To:

From:

Date:

THE HOPE of CHRISTMAS

JACK COUNTRYMAN

A Division of Thomas Nelson Publishers

THOMAS NELSON
Since 1798

NASHVILLE   DALLAS   MEXICO CITY   RIO DE JANEIRO

The Hope of Christmas

Published in Nashville, Tennessee, by Thomas Nelson. Thomas Nelson is a registered trademark of Thomas Nelson, Inc.

Italics in Scripture indicate the author's emphasis.

Scripture quotations are taken from the NEW KING JAMES VERSION © 1982 by Thomas Nelson, Inc. Used by permission. All rights reserved.

Thomas Nelson, Inc., titles may be purchased in bulk for educational, business, fund-raising, or sales promotional use. For information, please e-mail SpecialMarkets@ThomasNelson.com.

ISBN-13: 978-1-4003-2114-8

Printed in China

12 13 14 15 16 RRD 5 4 3 2 1

www.thomasnelson.com

God makes a promise.

Faith believes His promise.

Hope anticipates its fulfillment.

Patience quietly waits.

Contents

The Christmas Story

*I*t's a timeless story—the account of Jesus' birth— with familiar details such as shepherds, a star, wise men, and angels. But perhaps the details, if not the story itself, are too familiar. Are we any longer able to hear the wonder of this world-changing, history-altering story?

God planned the birth of Jesus before time began, and throughout the Old Testament—thousands of years before a Baby was born in Bethlehem—God hinted about the coming of this Messiah, this King of kings, Lord of lords, Prince of Peace.

Looking at these hints—these ancient prophecies— and their fulfillment in the New Testament accounts of Jesus' birth can help us recapture the wonder of the Christmas story and marvel at the gift of Jesus, a gift of sacrifice and love, of Immanuel, "God with us."

May seeing the promises of God and their fulfillment reignite in you the very *hope of Christmas.*

It came to pass in those days that a decree went out from Caesar Augustus that all the world should be registered. This census first took place while Quirinius was governing Syria. So all went to be registered, everyone to his own city.

Joseph also went up from Galilee, out of the city of Nazareth, into Judea, to the city of David, which is called Bethlehem, because he was of the house and lineage of David, to be registered with Mary, his betrothed wife, who was with child. So it was, that while they were there, the days were completed for her to be delivered. And she brought forth her firstborn Son, and wrapped Him in swaddling cloths, and laid Him in a manger, because there was no room for them in the inn.

Now there were in the same country shepherds living out in the fields, keeping watch over their flock by night. And behold, an angel of the Lord stood before them, and the glory of the Lord shone around them, and they were greatly afraid. Then the angel said to them, "Do not be afraid, for behold, I bring you good tidings of great joy which will be to all people. For there is born to you this day in the city of David a Savior, who is Christ the Lord. And this will be the sign to you: You will find a Babe wrapped in swaddling cloths, lying in a manger."

And suddenly there was with the angel a multitude of the heavenly host praising God and saying:

> *"Glory to God in the highest,*
> *And on earth peace,*
> *goodwill toward men!"*

Luke 2:1–14

Introduction

For centuries, voices in the Old Testament called God's people to look for the Messiah, yet most Jewish people missed the significance of the prophets' words. Micah, for instance, said the Messiah would be born in Bethlehem. In Psalm 89:27, 36, David foretold of a firstborn when he spoke of the Lord declaring that David's seed would endure forever. Isaiah made the preposterous claim that the Messiah would be born of a virgin. Hosea revealed that at a certain time God would call His Son out of Egypt. Such Old Testament prophecies and promises were spoken five hundred to seven hundred years *before* the birth of Christ, and devout Jews would wonder, "Will the Messiah come in my lifetime? Will I see the Promised One with my own eyes?"

In a sense, when we open God's Word today, we see with our own eyes as well as the eyes of our hearts that all of God's promises regarding the Anointed One of God are fulfilled, detail for detail, in the life of Jesus of Nazareth.

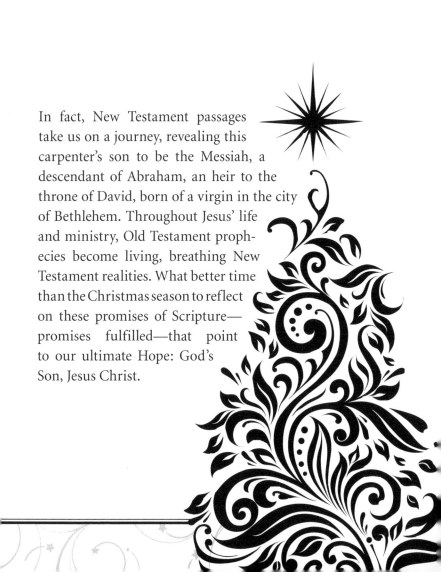

In fact, New Testament passages take us on a journey, revealing this carpenter's son to be the Messiah, a descendant of Abraham, an heir to the throne of David, born of a virgin in the city of Bethlehem. Throughout Jesus' life and ministry, Old Testament prophecies become living, breathing New Testament realities. What better time than the Christmas season to reflect on these promises of Scripture—promises fulfilled—that point to our ultimate Hope: God's Son, Jesus Christ.

Messiah, Descendant of Abraham

Now the LORD had said to Abram:
"Get out of your country,
From your family
And from your father's house,
To a land that I will show you.
I will make you a great nation;
I will bless you
And make your name great;
And you shall be a blessing.
I will bless those who bless you,
And I will curse him who curses you;
And in you all the families of the earth shall
*   be blessed."*

So Abram departed as the LORD had spoken to
him, and Lot went with him. And Abram was seventy-
five years old when he departed from Haran.

Genesis 12:1–4

*W*hat an amazing promise! The Creator of the universe chose to make this everlasting and irrevocable promise to Abraham and his descendants. Speaking these words recorded in Genesis, the Almighty pointed to the greatest blessing of all, a blessing that would be for all the earth: God would give His Son to die for sinners like us, that we might know forgiveness and eternal life. Through two thousand years and forty-two generations, a new chapter in the sovereign Lord's plan for humanity was beginning to unfold—and all the families of the earth would indeed be blessed.

Genealogy of Jesus

The book of the genealogy of Jesus Christ, the Son of David, the Son of Abraham. . . . So all the generations from Abraham to David are fourteen generations, from David until the captivity in Babylon are fourteen generations, and from the captivity in Babylon until the Christ are fourteen generations.

Matthew 1:1, 17

*P*romise made, promise fulfilled! Writing to a primarily Jewish audience, Matthew outlined Jesus' ancestry. The gospel writer wanted his Hebrew audience to clearly see that Jesus was indeed the long-awaited King of Israel, in the line of David, who would set God's people free from captivity to sin and its consequences.

Yet Matthew did something unusual as he outlined the family tree. He named five *women*: Tamar, a Canaanite; Rahab, a Gentile; Ruth, a Moabite; Bathsheba, King David's wife; and Mary, the teenage mother of Jesus. Why? Because their stories, recorded in the Old Testament, demonstrate that God's grace is available to all, regardless of gender, race, or personal history. In fact, even today God seems to delight in welcoming into His family those we might never expect.

This season, keep your eyes and heart open for unexpected ways that God will reveal to you the hope of Christmas.

His Blessing

~~~ ✳ ~~~

*When God made a promise to Abraham, because
He could swear by no one greater, He swore by
Himself, saying, "Surely blessing I will bless you, and
multiplying I will multiply you." And so, after he
had patiently endured, he obtained the promise.*

Hebrews 6:13–15

Our God loves to pour out blessings! He demonstrates His love to those of us who love Him—who show our love by obeying Him—when He provides and protects, when He guides our steps and goes ahead of us, when He walks with us through hard times and brings us to good and pleasant places. God blesses us with His constant presence. Whatever trials we face, nothing can separate us from His love. Whatever twists in the road, nothing can interfere with His sovereign power and goodness. Whatever missteps we take, He can redeem. Whatever hurts we experience, He can heal. Yes, our God loves to pour out blessings!

Blessed is the man
Who walks not in the counsel of the ungodly,
Nor stands in the path of sinners,
Nor sits in the seat of the scornful;
But his delight is in the law of the LORD,
And in His law he meditates day and night.
He shall be like a tree
Planted by the rivers of water,
That brings forth its fruit in its
season,
Whose leaf also shall not wither;
And whatever he does shall prosper.

Psalm 1:1–3

Heir to the Throne of David

—❋—

For unto us a Child is born,
Unto us a Son is given;
And the government will be upon His shoulder.
And His name will be called
Wonderful, Counselor, Mighty God,
Everlasting Father, Prince of Peace.
Of the increase of His government and peace
There will be no end,
Upon the throne of David and over His kingdom,
To order it and establish it with judgment and
justice
From that time forward, even forever.
The zeal of the LORD of hosts will perform this.

Isaiah 9:6–7

What nation wouldn't want a leader described as "Wonderful, Counselor, Mighty God, Everlasting Father, Prince of Peace"? No wonder the people of Israel, oppressed by the brutal Roman Empire, found in this 750-year-old passage by the prophet Isaiah hope for a military conqueror and deliverer. But these ancient words actually point to a much bigger plan—to the Lord's eternal strategy for conquering sin and delivering sinners from the unbridgeable distance between them and their holy God. And of the increase of His government and our peace with Him there will be no end!

Gabriel Visits Mary

~ ✳ ~

Then the angel said to her, "Do not be afraid, Mary,
for you have found favor with God. And behold, you
will conceive in your womb and bring forth a Son,
and shall call His name JESUS. He will be great, and
will be called the Son of the Highest; and the Lord
God will give Him the throne of His father David.
And He will reign over the house of Jacob forever,
and of His kingdom there will be no end."

Luke 1:30–33

Fulfillment

*A*n unremarkable day would soon become unforgettable for this young girl named Mary. Maybe she was grinding grain or mending a garment when, suddenly, a light appeared and an angel spoke. She was terrified.

"Do not be afraid," the angel told her as his message actually became quite fearsome.

Although she was an unmarried virgin, Mary would give birth to the Son of God. Gabriel went on to reveal that the child would be a descendant of David and that His kingdom would never end.

And so Mary waited for the miracle . . .

God's Promise to Mary

"Blessed is she who believed, for there will be a fulfillment of those things which were told her from the Lord."

And Mary said:
> *"My soul magnifies the Lord,*
> *And my spirit has rejoiced in God my Savior.*
> *For He has regarded the lowly state of His*
> > *maidservant;*
> *For behold, henceforth all generations will*
> > *call me blessed.*
> *For He who is mighty has done great things for me,*
> *And holy is His name.*
> *And His mercy is on those who fear Him*
> *From generation to generation.*
> *He has shown strength with His arm;*
> *He has scattered the proud in the imagination of*
> > *their hearts.*
> *He has put down the mighty from their thrones,*
> *And exalted the lowly.*

He has filled the hungry with good things,
And the rich He has sent away empty.
He has helped His servant Israel,
In remembrance of His mercy,
As He spoke to our fathers,
To Abraham and to his seed forever."

Luke 1:45–55

From all appearances, Mary was an ordinary girl living in a one-stop-light town—when an amazing moment revealed both her extraordinary character and her uncommon faith in her unseen and ever-faithful God. Believing the angel's outrageous claim that she would give birth to God's Son and completely trusting that the Almighty would enable her to walk that path, Mary yielded her life—her very body—to her Creator. Despite the cost to her, despite the public shame and her derailed dreams, Mary was a model of humble and willing submission to the Lord's plans, and the world has celebrated her obedience to God for more than two thousand years.

AWAY
in a
MANGER

ANONYMOUS

Away in a manger, no crib for a bed,
The little Lord Jesus laid down His sweet head.
The stars in the sky look down where He lay,
The little Lord Jesus, asleep on the hay.

The cattle are lowing, the baby awakes
But little Lord Jesus, no crying He makes.
I love Thee, Lord Jesus; look down from the
sky,
And stay by my cradle till morning is nigh.

Be near me, Lord Jesus; I ask Thee to stay
Close by me forever and love me, I pray.
Bless all the dear children in Thy tender care,
And take us to heaven to live with Thee there.

Anointed and Eternal

~~ ✴ ~~

Your throne, O God, is forever and ever;
A scepter of righteousness is the scepter of Your
*   kingdom.*
You love righteousness and hate wickedness;
Therefore God, Your God, has anointed You
With the oil of gladness more than Your
*   companions.*

Psalm 45:6–7

An unmistakable sense of joy fills the air. The crowd's excited anticipation is unmistakable. Everyone in the realm is joining in this celebration of the King's reign. The almighty God has anointed Jesus, our Savior, to rule—with justice and uprightness—over all history.

As He reigns for eternity with unwavering and holy righteousness, King Jesus will bring joy and gladness to His people and, more important, glory and honor to His Father. The King of kings and Lord of lords will come as a Bridegroom seeking His bride to reign forever with joy and gladness.

Unchanging

---※---

"You, LORD, in the beginning laid the founda-
  tion of the earth,
And the heavens are the work of Your hands.
They will perish, but You remain;
And they will all grow old like a garment;
Like a cloak You will fold them up,
And they will be changed.
But You are the same."

Hebrews 1:10–12

From the beginning of time, Jesus has been present. He was with the Father and the Spirit when the earth was formed and the waters were separated from the land. Through the millennia, landforms have changed; in the course of a year, seasons come and go.

In contrast to this constant change, Jesus has remained and will forever remain the same: holy, good, strong, loving, faithful, powerful, and wise. So as the events of the world and the details of life whirl around you, know that Jesus will not change. He is a Rock, and He will never fail you.

The Word Became Flesh

~~~ ✳ ~~~

*H*ave you ever received a one-of-a-kind gift? Something unique, completely unlike anything you had ever seen or even heard of? When the apostle John referred to Jesus as the "only begotten of the Father," the original Greek means "unique" or "one-of-a-kind." And as God's gift to us, Jesus—who is both fully God and fully man—is indeed unique.

Yet, as the Lamb of God who died on the cross on behalf of sinful humanity, Jesus is not a gift to be hoarded. What will you do to share your one-of-a-kind gift of Jesus with someone this season?

In the beginning was the Word, and the Word was with God, and the Word was God. He was in the beginning with God. All things were made through Him, and without Him nothing was made that was made. In Him was life, and the life was the light of men. And the light shines in the darkness, and the darkness did not comprehend it. . . . And the Word became flesh and dwelt among us, and we beheld His glory, the glory as of the only begotten of the Father, full of grace and truth.

John 1:1–5, 14

Watch Bethlehem

"But you, Bethlehem Ephrathah,
Though you are little among the thousands of
Judah,
Yet out of you shall come forth to Me
The One to be Ruler in Israel,
Whose goings forth are from of old,
From everlasting."
Therefore He shall give them up,
Until the time that she who is in labor has given
birth;
Then the remnant of His brethren
Shall return to the children of Israel.
And He shall stand and feed His flock
In the strength of the Lord,
In the majesty of the name of the Lord *His God;*
And they shall abide,
For now He shall be great
To the ends of the earth;
And this One shall be peace.

When the Assyrian comes into our land,
And when he treads in our palaces,
Then we will raise against him
Seven shepherds and eight princely men."

Micah 5:2–5

*I*ts name means "house of bread." It had been renowned as the City of David. Yet by Jesus' time, Bethlehem had become a humble town, small and seemingly insignificant. However, in that unassuming town, the prophet Micah said, the Messiah would be born. Micah's message to God's people was this: "Watch! Something important is going to happen in Bethlehem!" Would people listen? Would Micah be right? Would the Bread of Life indeed come into this world in the "house of bread"?

Born in Bethlehem

Joseph also went up from Galilee, out of the city of Nazareth, into Judea, to the city of David, which is called Bethlehem, because he was of the house and lineage of David, to be registered with Mary, his betrothed wife, who was with child. So it was, that while they were there, the days were completed for her to be delivered. And she brought forth her firstborn Son, and wrapped Him in swaddling cloths, and laid Him in a manger, because there was no room for them in the inn.

Luke 2:4–7

Fulfillment

*T*he journey had been commanded by Rome. Joseph the carpenter and Mary, his betrothed, would cover the ninety miles in about three days. The young woman was exceedingly pregnant, and when they arrived, Bethlehem was crowded to its limits. Yet—as Micah had foretold long ago—Mary and Joseph were in Bethlehem when the Savior of the world broke forth from Mary's womb.

The young couple had been directed to a nearby stable, and there Mary gave birth to her firstborn Son, wrapped Him in swaddling cloths, and placed Him in a feeding trough. God's one and only Son had entered our dark and sinful world.

The Gift of Jesus the Messiah

～※～

*T*he Son of God, eternal throughout time, infinite in every way, entered the confines of a twenty-four-hour day and the finiteness of a human body in order to dwell among us. And He would do more—far more—than visit and observe. Jesus left His Father's side, took on human flesh, and walked among us in order to die for us.

And God had spoken through prophets to call people to watch for the coming Messiah. He sent angels to announce Jesus' birth, and Jesus revealed His identity through His signs and miracles and teaching—and His death and resurrection. Yet many people missed Him—and still miss Him today.

The night our Savior was born in Bethlehem was a night like many others before it—but unlike any night since. Would you have recognized its significance? And whom will you help recognize it even now, two thousand years later?

He is the image of the invisible God, the firstborn over all creation. For by Him all things were created that are in heaven and that are on earth, visible and invisible, whether thrones or dominions or principalities or powers. All things were created through Him and for Him. And He is before all things, and in Him all things consist. And He is the head of the body, the church, who is the beginning, the firstborn from the dead, that in all things He may have the preeminence.

Colossians 1:15–18

O LITTLE TOWN of BETHLEHEM

PHILLIPS BROOKS

O little town of Bethlehem, how still we see thee lie;
Above thy deep and dreamless sleep the silent stars
go by.
Yet in thy dark streets shineth the everlasting Light;
The hopes and fears of all the years are met in thee
tonight.

For Christ is born of Mary and gathered all above;
While mortals sleep the angels keep their watch of
wondering love.
O morning stars together proclaim the holy birth;
And praises sing to God the King and peace to men
on earth.

How silently, how silently, the wondrous gift is giv'n;
So God imparts to human hearts the blessings of His
heaven.
No ear may hear His coming, but in this world of sin,
Where meek souls will receive Him still, the dear
Christ enters in.

O holy Child of Bethlehem, descend to us we pray;
Cast out our sin and enter in; be born in us today.
We hear the Christmas angels, the great glad
tidings tell;
O come to us, abide with us, Our Lord, Emmanuel!

Born of a Virgin

The Lord Himself will give you a sign: Behold, the virgin shall conceive and bear a Son, and shall call His name Immanuel.

Isaiah 7:14

The wolf also shall dwell with the lamb,
The leopard shall lie down with the young goat,
The calf and the young lion and the fatling
*   together;*
And a little child shall lead them.

Isaiah 11:6

*I*t is an age-old story perhaps best brought to life by the youngest of Christ's followers. In churches across the land, the birth of Jesus will be celebrated by the shepherd wearing his oversized bathrobe and holding his too-small crook; Mary, draped in blue and busying herself with her favorite, now swaddled, doll; the king from the east waving to Mom, who snaps pictures from the first pew; the lamb from the three-year-old class wandering around the makeshift crèche as lambs do; and Joseph, looking like he'd rather be anywhere but on stage!

As Isaiah wrote when he was describing the righteous kingdom Jesus will one day establish, "a little child shall lead" (11:6)—and children do indeed lead us to the manger at Christmas!

Highly Favored One

Now in the sixth month the angel Gabriel was sent by God to a city of Galilee named Nazareth, to a virgin betrothed to a man whose name was Joseph, of the house of David. The virgin's name was Mary. And having come in, the angel said to her, "Rejoice, highly favored one, the Lord is with you; blessed are you among women!"

But when she saw him, she was troubled at his saying, and considered what manner of greeting this was. Then the angel said to her, "Do not be afraid, Mary, for you have found favor with God. And behold, you will conceive in your womb and bring forth a Son, and shall call His name JESUS. He will be great, and will be called the Son of the Highest; and the Lord God will give Him the throne of His father David. And He will reign over the house of Jacob forever, and of His kingdom there will be no end."

Luke 1:26–33

*G*od's ways aren't our ways, and the plan of Christmas might have had even the angel Gabriel scratching his head.

> What a privilege to share the news that the long-awaited Messiah is about to walk the darkened earth! But I certainly didn't expect a young woman—actually, still a girl—to be the first one to hear the news, much less be the one to give birth to the Almighty's only Son. And to think she lives in Nazareth. I've heard it said, "Can anything good come from Nazareth?" Now something—Someone—wonderful beyond words is.

Mary was upset by the angel's sudden and glorious appearance, so after he greeted her, Gabriel said, "Do not be afraid" (Luke 1:30). Somewhat reassured, Mary listened, asked a few questions, and then set an example of godly submission and trust: "I am the Lord's servant. May it be to me as you have said" (v. 38).

May we follow the example of this one chosen by God.

Immanuel, "God with Us"

～❋～

*S*he was favored; we are blessed. Mary yielded her life, her dreams, her very body to the Sovereign and His plan for all humanity. The Holy God, who had been immeasurably far away since our first mother and father sinned in the garden, would come to earth through young Mary's holy womb and be Immanuel, "God with us."

Some people will make their annual or semi-annual visit to church in honor of this God who has come near. But if this Babe truly is God, does He not deserve more attention than Christmas Eve and perhaps Easter Sunday? Jesus has come close for a reason. Actually, for several reasons. He wants His wandering sheep—sinful human beings—to recognize their sin, receive His forgiveness, and live with Him, now and for eternity, as Lord of their lives. Jesus has come near to bless us with His grace, to guide us, protect us, provide for us, to free us from our sinful ways and their consequences, to show us and tell us that He loves us.

Receive Jesus' love if you haven't. Share His love if you have.

So all this was done that it might be fulfilled which was spoken by the Lord through the prophet, saying: "Behold, the virgin shall be with child, and bear a Son, and they shall call His name Immanuel," which is translated, "God with us."

Matthew 1:22–23

O COME,
O Come,
EMMANUEL

NINTH-CENTURY LATIN HYMN
TRANSLATED BY JOHN M. NEALE

O come, O come, Emmanuel,
And ransom captive Israel,
That mourns in lonely exile here
Until the Son of God appear.

Rejoice! Rejoice! Emmanuel
Shall come to thee, O Israel!

O come, Thou Wisdom from on high,
Who orderest all things mightily;
To us the path of knowledge show
And teach us in her ways to go.

Rejoice! Rejoice! Emmanuel
Shall come to thee, O Israel!

O come, Desire of nations, bind
In one the hearts of all mankind.
Bid Thou our sad divisions cease,
And be Thyself our King of Peace.

Rejoice! Rejoice! Emmanuel
Shall come to thee, O Israel!

O come, thou Dayspring, come and cheer
Our spirits by Thine advent here;
Disperse the gloomy clouds of night,
And death's dark shadows put to flight.

Rejoice! Rejoice! Emmanuel
Shall come to thee, O Israel!

The Messenger

"Behold, I send My messenger,
And he will prepare the way before Me.
And the Lord, whom you seek,
Will suddenly come to His temple,
Even the Messenger of the covenant,
In whom you delight.
Behold, He is coming,"
Says the LORD of hosts.
"But who can endure the day of His coming?
And who can stand when He appears?
For He is like a refiner's fire
And like launderers' soap.
He will sit as a refiner and a purifier of silver;
He will purify the sons of Levi,
And purge them as gold and silver,
That they may offer to the LORD
An offering in righteousness."

Malachi 3:1–3

*I*n this age of television, radio, the Internet, texting, and social media, human messengers are rarely required to share any breaking or important news. But Old Testament events occurred long before these twenty-first-century wonders, and Malachi, whose name means "My messenger," delivered God's plea to His people: "Turn back to Me!" The dramatic wording—"Behold, He is coming"—implied that the arrival would be imminent, but His coming wouldn't actually take place for another four hundred years.

Speaking on behalf of God the Father, Malachi prophesied about the coming of the Lord Jesus. The *human* messenger Malachi mentioned is John the Baptist, and in this prophecy, "the *Lord*" and "the Messenger of the covenant" refer to Jesus.

To whom will you—like Malachi—be a messenger this holy season and share the news that Jesus Christ is born?

The Messenger Comes

When the messengers of John had departed, [Jesus] began to speak to the multitudes concerning John: "What did you go out into the wilderness to see? A reed shaken by the wind? But what did you go out to see? A man clothed in soft garments? Indeed those who are gorgeously appareled and live in luxury are in kings' courts. But what did you go out to see? A prophet? Yes, I say to you, and more than a prophet. This is he of whom it is written:

> *'Behold, I send My messenger before Your face, Who will prepare Your way before You.'*

"For I say to you, among those born of women there is not a greater prophet than John the Baptist; but he who is least in the kingdom of God is greater than he."

Luke 7:24–28

*I*n Jesus' day, a king's envoys would go before him, making the way safe and announcing his coming. Before Jesus began His public ministry, John the Baptist went before Him, announcing His coming with a call to repentance and baptism. After four hundred years of God's silence—of no prophetic voice speaking on the Lord's behalf—the people of Israel were eager to hear God's message spoken by John, the self-proclaimed fulfillment of Malachi's prophecy.

Like John, you and I can testify to the coming of Jesus—His first coming to defeat sin and death and His Second Coming to establish His eternal kingdom. You and I can be messengers of this truth, of this good news, or gospel. As Saint Francis of Assisi said to believers, "Preach the gospel at all times. If necessary use words."

Spiritual Gifts and Talents

～※～

*J*ohn the Baptist obeyed God's calling to be the messenger who led people to repent and be baptized. Obedient to this calling, John was faithful to the point of losing his life rather than backing down. To God be the glory!

God is still glorified when, like John the Baptist, His people use their spiritual gifts "for the profit of all." God works in each individual to benefit the entire body. And although different tasks within the body call for different gifts, all tasks and gifts have the same goal. At the time when each of us comes to faith in Christ, we receive at least one gift—not merely to build up our own life of faith but also to strengthen unity in the church. Ask God today to show you the gifts and talents given to you by His Spirit. Then use those gifts in the body of Christ as He directs. As you do so, you'll find your faith stretched and strengthened.

There are diversities of gifts, but the same Spirit. There are differences of ministries, but the same Lord. And there are diversities of activities, but it is the same God who works all in all. But the manifestation of the Spirit is given to each one for the profit of all: for to one is given the word of wisdom through the Spirit, to another the word of knowledge through the same Spirit, to another faith by the same Spirit, to another gifts of healings by the same Spirit, to another the working of miracles, to another prophecy, to another discerning of spirits, to another different kinds of tongues, to another the interpretation of tongues. But one and the same Spirit works all these things, distributing to each one individually as He wills.

1 Corinthians 12:4–11

The Son of God

Prophecy

"Yet I have set My King
On My holy hill of Zion.
I will declare the decree:
The LORD has said to Me,
'You are My Son,
Today I have begotten You.
Ask of Me, and I will give You
The nations for Your inheritance,
And the ends of the earth for Your possession.
You shall break them with a rod of iron;
You shall dash them to pieces like a potter's
    vessel.'"

Psalm 2:6–9

*T*he plane came to a stop at the boarding gate. Stepping off the plane, the young boy took a deep breath before starting through the hallway. As he entered the lobby, he looked around timidly. Then, there in the crowd (and much to his relief), he saw the smile of the one who was now his father. What joy overcame both father and son!

Since ancient times and up to the present day, an adoption has been a cause for great and joyous celebration. At the same time, it is a serious event. From the time of David until the day of Jesus Himself, the phrase "You are My Son" was spoken over each legitimate descendant of David who was crowned king, signifying that the king was adopted by God as His "son" to rule with absolute authority. The newly crowned king would then look to God as his Father.

May you, as an adopted child of the King, look to the Almighty for direction and wisdom as well.

Jesus, God's Son

～✳～

When He had been baptized, Jesus came up immediately from the water; and behold, the heavens were opened to Him, and He saw the Spirit of God descending like a dove and alighting upon Him. And suddenly a voice came from heaven, saying, "This is My beloved Son, in whom I am well pleased."

Matthew 3:16–17

Fulfillment

At the very beginning of Jesus' earthly ministry—as John baptized Him—Jesus heard His Father's words of approval. The Holy Spirit descended "like a dove," and God spoke—in fulfillment of the Psalm 2:7 prophecy—"You are My Son."

In accordance with His Father's will, Jesus had gone to John the Baptist to be baptized. By doing so, Jesus not only validated John's ministry but also identified Himself with the sinful human beings whose punishment He would take upon Himself on the cross.

What wondrous love is this! Divine love affirms even when human love doesn't.

God's Favor

――※――

*W*hether we do someone a favor or show someone favor, we are freely giving of our love, our
time, our finances, our possessions. But giving freely
does not mean the gift itself was free. When God
shows us His favor—when He offers His forgiveness,
His love, His mercy, His grace, His protection, His
provision—He does so freely, but that favor did not
come cheap. It cost Jesus His life.

Having invested His own Son's life on our behalf,
God continually pours out His favor on those who
recognize the sacrifice of the cross. In the words of
the psalmist, God's favor "will surround [us] as with
a shield." Our loving God will bestow His favor upon
us through all of life's circumstances. As we receive
God's favor—during this blessed season and year-
round—may we find ways to share it with those
around us.

But let all those rejoice who put their trust in You;
Let them ever shout for joy, because You defend them;
Let those also who love Your name
Be joyful in You.
*For You, O L*ORD*, will bless the righteous;*
With favor You will surround him as with
   a shield.

Psalm 5:11–12

Blessed is the man who listens to me,
Watching daily at my gates,
Waiting at the posts of my doors.
For whoever finds me finds life,
*And obtains favor from the L*ORD*.*

Proverbs 8:34–35

Light from Galilee

The gloom will not be upon her who is distressed,
As when at first He lightly esteemed
The land of Zebulun and the land of Naphtali,
And afterward more heavily oppressed her,
By the way of the sea, beyond the Jordan,
In Galilee of the Gentiles.
The people who walked in darkness
Have seen a great light;
Those who dwelt in the land of the shadow of death,
Upon them a light has shined.

Isaiah 9:1–2

*O*ut on the sea, drifting along in the calm of night, a captain awaits the sunrise that will break the darkness. In a similar situation, Isaiah spoke this prophecy in anticipation of light after darkness, of an explosion of light and Good News. For thousands of years, the Jewish people had been looking for the King who would come, bring an end to war, and usher in universal peace. They were waiting for the sunrise that would shatter their darkness once and for all.

Ministry in Galilee

Jesus went about all Galilee, teaching in their synagogues, preaching the gospel of the kingdom, and healing all kinds of sickness and all kinds of disease among the people. . . . Great multitudes followed Him—from Galilee, and from Decapolis, Jerusalem, Judea, and beyond the Jordan.

Matthew 4:23, 25

When Jesus, hailing from Galiliee, walked this earth, His ministry of teaching, preaching, and healing fulfilled Isaiah's ancient prophecy. This God-man wanted people to recognize who had sent Him and then enter into a more intimate relationship with the Father. With words and healings, Jesus taught that an internal change of the heart was necessary before a sinner could enter into a true relationship with God. Jesus shined the light of this truth and others every day of His life, as did those—then and now—who came to follow Him.

What are you doing to let your light shine so that others might see Jesus in you?

God's Power

What a responsibility! How can flesh and bone—mere "earthen vessels"—possibly shine forth the glory of the living God? We can't—in our own power. But each day, as we faithfully serve Jesus, His Spirit works to mold us more and more into His image. As this process unfolds, people around us can see His light shining in us and through us, and we are able to be God's ambassadors in the world, used by Him to introduce people to the love and grace available to them in Christ. Acting in the power of the Holy Spirit, we can shine forth—in this season and always—the light of hope and joy for the good of those around us and for God's glory!

"Believe Me that I am in the Father and the Father in Me, or else believe Me for the sake of the works themselves. Most assuredly, I say to you, he who believes in Me, the works that I do he will do also; and greater works than these he will do, because I go to My Father. And whatever you ask in My name, that I will do, that the Father may be glorified in the Son."

John 14:11–13

For it is the God who commanded light to shine out of darkness, who has shone in our hearts to give the light of the knowledge of the glory of God in the face of Jesus Christ. But we have this treasure in earthen vessels, that the excellence of the power may be of God and not of us.

2 Corinthians 4:6–7

Message of Freedom

———— ✦ ————

"The Spirit of the Lord GOD is upon Me,
Because the LORD has anointed Me
To preach good tidings to the poor;
He has sent Me to heal the brokenhearted,
To proclaim liberty to the captives,
And the opening of the prison to those who are
          bound;
To proclaim the acceptable year of the LORD.
And the day of vengeance of our God;
To comfort all who mourn,
To console those who mourn in Zion,
To give them beauty for ashes,
The oil of joy for mourning,
The garment of praise for the spirit of heaviness;
That they may be called trees of righteousness,
The planting of the LORD, that He may be glori-
          fied."

Isaiah 61:1–3

*N*atural disasters, personal strife, painful relationships, inexplicable events—any one of these can bind us, making us feel captive to circumstances and even abandoned, if not totally forgotten, by God.

Such was the case of the Jews who were in exile from their homeland after Assyria conquered their kingdom. Bound by this vicious captor, God's weary people thought the Almighty had forgotten them. Then, into that seemingly hopeless setting, Isaiah spoke this prophecy and offered hope for the future. The prophet encouraged the people of Israel to look not at their current circumstances but toward the glorious future God had promised them, a future of good news, healing, and, yes, *freedom*.

Freedom Proclaimed

[Jesus] came to Nazareth, where He had been brought up. And as His custom was, He went into the synagogue on the Sabbath day, and stood up to read. And He was handed the book of the prophet Isaiah. And when He had opened the book, He found the place where it was written:

*"The Spirit of the L*ORD *is upon Me. . . ."*

Then He closed the book, and gave it back to the attendant and sat down. And the eyes of all who were in the synagogue were fixed on Him. And He began to say to them, "Today this Scripture is fulfilled in your hearing."

Luke 4:16–18, 20–21

*I*t was the Sabbath day in His hometown of Nazareth, and like any upstanding Jew, Jesus went to the synagogue. When He stood up to read, He was handed the book of Isaiah. After reading from chapter 61, Jesus sat down and told the bewildered crowd that *He*—Jesus Himself—was the fulfillment of this prophecy. This Man who had grown up in this town and played on its dusty streets made the bold and straightforward assertion that He was the promised Messiah. What an astonishing claim!

And not unexpectedly—Jesus Himself said, "No prophet is accepted in his own country" (v. 24)—His proclamation was met with disbelief and fury. How could this carpenter's son, whom the people of Nazareth had known since His birth, make such lofty claims? What could He possibly say in His defense?

Likewise, what can you say in defense of your beliefs that Jesus is God's Son, the risen Lord who proved victorious over sin and death? Even today, many people question Jesus' claims. Be prepared to "give a defense to everyone who asks you a reason for the hope that is in you" in Jesus (1 Peter 3:15)!

God's Comfort

———— ✳ ————

*H*ave you noticed that the best source of comfort is someone who has struggled with pain, sorrow, or loss? That is one reason why God offers His followers the gift of comfort, so that we can, in turn, give it to others. Yes, God sometimes allows tragedy to enter our lives, but He never intends for us to go through difficult times alone. Once we have— by God's grace—gone through a dark time, God calls us to offer comfort to the hurting people He puts in our path. Often that comfort is our mere presence, not "right" words. Our willingness to share the kind of comfort we have received reflects both our knowledge of our good God and our faith in Him.

And whether we are receiving or offering comfort, we can rely on the greatest Comforter of all, the Holy Spirit. Given to us by God, the Spirit is continually with us, willing to guide and empower us as we come alongside hurting people. Yes, our Redeemer-God is at work when He uses the comforted to comfort others!

Blessed be the God and Father of our Lord Jesus Christ, the Father of mercies and God of all comfort, who comforts us in all our tribulation, that we may be able to comfort those who are in any trouble, with the comfort with which we ourselves are comforted by God. For as the sufferings of Christ abound in us, so our consolation also abounds through Christ. Now if we are afflicted, it is for your consolation and salvation, which is effective for enduring the same sufferings which we also suffer. Or if we are comforted, it is for your consolation and salvation. And our hope for you is steadfast, because we know that as you are partakers of the sufferings, so also you will partake of the consolation.

2 Corinthians 1:3–7

Man of Sorrows

He is despised and rejected by men,
A Man of sorrows and acquainted with grief.
And we hid, as it were, our faces from Him;
He was despised, and we did not esteem Him.

Isaiah 53:3

Whether we're turned down for a date, not called back after an interview, ignored at a party, or brokenhearted when a relationship ends, rejection hurts—and we all experience it. Jesus Himself experienced rejection, just as Isaiah had prophesied about the Son of God, whom he referred to as a "Man of sorrows." That description doesn't mean that Jesus lacked humor or had a sour attitude. That phrase means that Jesus Himself experienced the kind of sorrow and rejection you have experienced. He knows your hurts because He has felt them too. He knows your grief and stands ready with open arms to comfort you.

Acceptance Through Jesus

He came to His own, and His own did not receive Him.

John 1:11

Whatever Jesus did or said and wherever He went, He encountered people who hoped to ruin His ministry and reputation. Instead of being welcomed and esteemed as the promised Messiah, Jesus regularly found Himself harshly questioned and ultimately rejected. Despite this opposition, Jesus continued to share God's unconditional love and forgiveness with all. The pains and denials of this world did not slow His efforts or quell His love. What comfort we find in the truth that Jesus will *never* turn His back on us or reject us.

Fulfillment

God's Goodness

The LORD is my shepherd;
I shall not want.
He makes me to lie down in green pastures;
He leads me beside the still waters.
He restores my soul;
He leads me in the paths of righteousness
For His name's sake.

Yea, though I walk through the valley of the
shadow of death,
I will fear no evil;
For You are with me;
Your rod and Your staff, they comfort me.

You prepare a table before me in the presence of
my enemies;
You anoint my head with oil;
My cup runs over.
Surely goodness and mercy shall follow me
All the days of my life;
And I will dwell in the house of the LORD
Forever.

Psalm 23

*S*urely goodness and mercy shall follow me all the days of my life"? Certain days—certain seasons of life—may cause us to question God's goodness, His mercy, and even His presence with us. In times like that, we choose to believe this truth David proclaimed. We choose to trust that God is with us and is choreographing good to come as a result of these dark places. We choose to believe—regardless of our circumstances—that Jesus, our Good Shepherd, is with us and is caring for us. After all, God promises us not just joy in His blessed presence for eternity but joy in this life as well. So choose to be aware of and to savor His goodness to you in this life. Thank Him continually for being your Good Shepherd, for knowing you by name, and for guiding your steps.

> *Oh, how great is Your goodness,*
> *Which You have laid up for those who*
>   *fear You,*
> *Which You have prepared for those*
>   *who trust in You*
> *In the presence of the sons of*
>   *men!*

Psalm 31:19

Hallelujah, What a Savior!

Philip P. Bliss

"Man of Sorrows!" what a name
For the Son of God who came
Ruined sinners to reclaim!
Hallelujah! What a Savior!

Bearing shame and scoffing rude,
In my place condemned He stood,
Sealed my pardon with His blood.
Hallelujah! What a Savior!

Guilty, vile, and helpless we;
Spotless Lamb of God was He;
Full atonement! Can it be?
Hallelujah! What a Savior!

Lifted up was He to die;
"It is finished!" was His cry;
Now in heaven exalted high.
Hallelujah! What a Savior!

When He comes, our glorious King,
All His ransomed home to bring,
Then anew this song we'll sing:
Hallelujah! What a Savior!

Portrait of a King

Who has believed our report?
And to whom has the arm of the Lord been
  revealed?
For He shall grow up before Him as a tender
  plant,
And as a root out of dry ground.
He has no form or comeliness;
And when we see Him,
There is no beauty that we should desire Him.
He is despised and rejected by men,
A Man of sorrows and acquainted with grief.
And we hid, as it were, our faces from Him;
He was despised, and we did not esteem Him.

Isaiah 53:1–3

*I*n these haunting verses, Isaiah painted a picture of the coming Messiah—and it's a rather unattractive picture. We read that the Promised One would be rejected and despised, dismissed rather than accepted and believed. And our Messiah was not the first of God's people to be treated that way. During the hundred years that Noah took to build the ark, he was ridiculed and harassed, yet he remained faithful to his God. Other figures in the Bible—think of Paul—were also rejected by men as they did God's will. So Isaiah's description of the Messiah should not surprise us. It seems that the more closely we follow God, the more opposition we encounter from unbelievers. And that is exactly what the prophet said God's own Son would face.

Jesus Was Not Believed

Although He had done so many signs before [the Jews], they did not believe in Him, that the word of Isaiah the prophet might be fulfilled, which he spoke:

> *"Lord, who has believed our report?*
> *And to whom has the arm of the LORD been*
> *revealed?"*

John 12:37–38

*W*hat is it about us human beings? We hear warnings, but we don't act—or we are surprised when the warnings prove accurate. A weather report alerts us to the vicious storm fast approaching, but when the clouds roll in and release their torrents, we are somehow still surprised.

Jesus, however, was not surprised when Isaiah's storm warnings proved true. Centuries before Jesus walked on this earth, the prophet said that the Messiah would come but not be believed—and that proved true. The people of Jesus' day had their own idea of what the Messiah would be like, and Jesus didn't match their expectations. Although some people did believe, Jesus was—as the prophet had spoken—rejected by many, and He was not surprised.

Even today people hear but reject the truth about Jesus. As storm warnings regarding His Second Coming circulate, people don't seem to care. In what ways does your life reflect your awareness that Jesus will return? And in what ways does your life reveal to others the truth that Jesus is your Savior and longs to be theirs?

His Faithfulness

——❋——

Let us hold fast the confession of our hope without wavering, for He who promised is faithful.

Hebrews 10:23

*I*n Hebrews 10:22, God invites us to "draw near" to Him with "a true heart in full assurance of faith." His invitation is grounded in the promise that He—our unchanging Lord—will always be faithful and that His love for us will absolutely never waver. We can therefore hold fast to the hope in our all-loving, all-powerful risen Lord, whose birth we celebrate this season. And may the hope that we have in Jesus Christ flavor our words and our actions so that others may see His grace and love and ask us about His faithfulness. May we have the opportunity this Christmas to share the story of Jesus' birth and the reasons for our hope in Him.

Forever, O Lord,
Your word is settled in heaven.
Your faithfulness endures to all generations;
You established the earth, and it abides.
They continue this day according to Your
ordinances,
For all are Your servants.

Psalm 119:89–91

Through the Lord's mercies we are not
consumed,
Because His compassions fail not.
They are new every morning;
Great is Your faithfulness.

Lamentations 3:22–23

GREAT
Is Thy
FAITHFULNESS

THOMAS O. CHISHOLM

Great is Thy faithfulness, O God my Father,
There is no shadow of turning with Thee;
Thou changest not, Thy compassions they
    fail not;
As Thou hast been Thou forever wilt be.

Summer and winter and springtime and
    harvest,
Sun, moon and stars in their courses above;
Join with all nature in manifold witness
To Thy great faithfulness, mercy and love.

Pardon for sin and a peace that endureth,
Thine own dear presence to cheer and
    to guide;
Strength for today and bright hope for
    tomorrow,
Blessings all mine, with ten thousand beside!

Great is Thy faithfulness! Great is Thy
    faithfulness!
Morning by morning new mercies I see;
All I have needed Thy hand hath provided;
Great is Thy faithfulness, Lord, unto me!

A Celebration

—✳—

Save now, I pray, O LORD;
O LORD, I pray, send now prosperity.
Blessed is he who comes in the name of the
    LORD!
We have blessed you from the house of the LORD.
God is the LORD,
And He has given us light;
Bind the sacrifice with cords to the horns of the
    altar.
You are my God, and I will praise You;
You are my God, I will exalt You.

Oh, give thanks to the LORD, for He is good!
For His mercy endures forever.

Psalm 118:25–29

When we need help—whether we need a little bit of assistance or an all-out rescue—we will cry out to someone who can deliver and who will come through with what we need. Similarly, in verse 25, the psalmist cries out to his God, who alone is able to save. Having spent twenty-four verses praising the Lord and thanking Him for earlier deliverance, the psalmist pleads for deliverance from his current circumstances. The song that has celebrated God's saving grace, unwavering faithfulness, and enduring love becomes prophetic in anticipation of God once again responding to His people's cry. Who would come "in the name of the Lord" to deliver him?

"Comes in the Name of the Lord"

A very great multitude spread their clothes on the road; others cut down branches from the trees and spread them on the road. Then the multitudes who went before and those who followed cried out, saying:

> *"Hosanna to the Son of David!*
> *'Blessed is He who comes in the name of the*
> *Lord!'*
> *Hosanna in the highest!"*

And when He had come into Jerusalem, all the city was moved, saying, "Who is this?"

So the multitudes said, "This is Jesus, the prophet from Nazareth of Galilee."

Matthew 21:8–11

*I*t was not the usual mode of transportation for a king, that young donkey Jesus rode into Jerusalem. And the less-than-majestic entrance was witnessed not by people of position and power, but by humble Jews who nevertheless cut palm fronds and spread them on the ground for Jesus to ride over, a practice normally reserved for a royal procession and people deserving great honor. And the crowd welcomed their Messiah and King with shouts of praise: "Hosanna to the Son of David!" and "Blessed is He who comes in the name of the Lord!" Yes, He was coming, a prophecy fulfilled, and the fulfillment had visibly begun in Bethlehem three decades earlier.

Unchanging God

~ ✳ ~

*W*hat Christmas traditions do you enjoy? Maybe you always bake cookies, decorate the tree at a specific time, or read the Christmas story before you open gifts—and maybe you've been doing these things for years, if not generations. But maybe some traditions have changed with time. The rich, buttery cookies Great-Grandma baked have been replaced by healthier oatmeal bars, or the tree gets decorated whenever a large group of family members is under the roof at the same time.

Unlike some of our Christmas traditions, our God does not change from year to year, from generation to generation, or even from century to century. He who came as a Baby to the manger in Bethlehem still comes to us—as risen King—whatever our humble circumstances. May we, in turn, go out to others in His name to share His love and grace.

Praise the LORD, all you Gentiles!
Laud Him, all you peoples!
For His merciful kindness is great toward us,
And the truth of the LORD endures forever.
Praise the LORD!

Psalm 117:1–2

Blessed be the name of the LORD
From this time forth and forevermore!
From the rising of the sun to its going
    down
The LORD's name is to be praised.
The LORD is high above all nations,
His glory above the heavens.

Psalm 113:2–4

A Trusted Friend?

—※—

All who hate me whisper together against me;
Against me they devise my hurt.
"An evil disease," they say, "clings to him.
And now that he lies down, he will rise up no
*   more."*
Even my own familiar friend in whom I trusted,
Who ate my bread,
Has lifted up his heel against me.

Psalm 41:7–9

*B*etrayed by a friend . . . Kicked while you were down . . . Lied to by someone you trusted . . . Left behind by a longtime ally . . . Left alone by a formerly faithful confidant . . .

David knew what you have felt, and his lament foreshadowed—his words in this psalm prophesied—what Jesus Himself would experience one day. Just as David and perhaps you yourself experienced, one of Jesus' close companions, someone who dined with Him, would betray Him. Learn from the example of David and, later, of your Lord, who went to the garden to pray. Reach out to God for solace. God will lift you up.

Dinner with Friends

～ ✳ ～

When evening had come, He sat down with the twelve. Now as they were eating, He said, "Assuredly, I say to you, one of you will betray Me."

And they were exceedingly sorrowful, and each of them began to say to Him, "Lord, is it I?"

He answered and said, "He who dipped his hand with Me in the dish will betray Me."

Matthew 26:20–23

"I do not speak concerning all of you. I know whom I have chosen; but that the Scripture may be fulfilled, 'He who eats bread with Me has lifted up his heel against Me.'"

John 13:18

Fulfillment

At the dinner table, looking around at each of His closest friends, Jesus' heart was heavy. He knew what the next twenty-four hours held for Him—and for His followers.

Well, all but one of them . . .

All except that one trusted disciple who had traveled with Jesus throughout His entire ministry, witnessed all of His miracles, and heard all of His teaching. This disciple, named Judas, would soon betray his Friend for thirty pieces of silver, at that time the price of a slave. Jesus looked at Judas, broke bread with him, and then sent him away to "lift up his heel" against Him. The prophecy of Psalm 41? Fulfilled.

His Grace

—※—

*A*re you on a quest for that perfect gift for someone you love? If so, you are undoubtedly considering personality, likes, dislikes—and your budget. You may be spending hours, if not days, going from website to website, store to store, sale to sale, trying to find exactly what you're looking for. Why? Because you love that person. Because of the joy you'll experience when you give the gift!

God already has the perfect gift for you, and it is . . . grace. It is a perfect fit. No exchanges are necessary. And it is unique: it comes only from Him through Jesus. In His grace, God accepts you not for who you are or what you have or haven't done, but because of who He is and what He allowed Jesus to do on the cross on your behalf. Yes, it's the perfect gift.

By grace you have been saved through faith, and that not of yourselves; it is the gift of God, not of works, lest anyone should boast. For we are His workmanship, created in Christ Jesus for good works, which God prepared beforehand that we should walk in them.

Ephesians 2:8–10

The Lord God is a sun and shield;
The Lord will give grace and glory;
No good thing will He withhold
From those who walk uprightly.
O Lord of hosts,
Blessed is the man who trusts in
You!

Psalm 84:11–12

AMAZING

Grace

JOHN NEWTON

Amazing grace! How sweet the sound!
That saved a wretch like me!
I once was lost, but now am found;
Was blind, but now I see.

'Twas grace that taught my heart to fear,
And grace my fears relieved.
How precious did that grace appear
The hour I first believed.

Thro' many dangers, toils and snares
I have already come.
'Tis grace that brought me safe thus far,
And grace will lead me home.

When we've been there ten thousand years,
Bright shining as the sun,
We've no less days to sing God's praise
Than when we've first begun.

Silence Is Golden

All we like sheep have gone astray;
We have turned, every one, to his own way;
And the LORD has laid on Him the iniquity
    of us all.
He was oppressed and He was afflicted,
Yet He opened not His mouth;
He was led as a lamb to the slaughter,
And as a sheep before its shearers is silent,
So He opened not His mouth.
He was taken from prison and from judgment,
And who will declare His generation?
For He was cut off from the land of the living;
For the transgressions of My people He was
    stricken.

Isaiah 53:6–8

*H*ave you ever been falsely accused of something? If so, you've undoubtedly wanted to shout your innocence and tell your side of the story. No one wants a reputation soiled or punishment without cause. Yet Isaiah prophesied that exactly this would happen to the Messiah. Isaiah described the wrongful accusations our Lord would face and compared Jesus to a lamb being brought to slaughter, an image his people knew all too well. It was a daily Jewish custom to kill a lamb as a sin offering, a peace offering to God. And according to this ancient prophecy, the Lamb of God—falsely accused—would be led to slaughter, submitting to God's plan of sacrifice and saying absolutely nothing in His own defense.

Silence Speaks Volumes

Now Jesus stood before the governor. And the governor asked Him, saying, "Are You the King of the Jews?"

Jesus said to him, "It is as you say." And while He was being accused by the chief priests and elders, He answered nothing.

Then Pilate said to Him, "Do You not hear how many things they testify against You?" But He answered him not one word, so that the governor marveled greatly.

Matthew 27:11–14

Fulfillment

When something bad happens, do you ever question God? Or maybe you cry out, "This isn't right or fair, God. I didn't sign up for this! Do something!"

Consider what Jesus might have felt like saying when He was questioned by the Jewish religious leaders and Roman rulers. The accusations against Him were unjust, inaccurate, and insufficient for the death sentence He ultimately received. The officials could find nothing substantial with which to charge Jesus. That being the case, we can probably think of a few things that we—and almost anyone else—would have said!

But Jesus was not like us. He knew that the events about to unfold were God's plan—and that He needed to allow this particular situation to play out—so Jesus remained silent. Prophecy fulfilled.

God's Guidance

~~~ ✳ ~~~

*A*lthough Jesus remained silent during His kangaroo-court trials, God Himself is not silent. He speaks through Scripture, He comforts by His Spirit, and He will guide continually and satisfy our souls when we choose to walk with Him through life. What a wonderful promise!

The Lord also promises that when we trust in Him with all our heart and allow Him to direct our lives, He will always go before us. The Holy Spirit is our source of truth, and He is with us and within us to guide our steps. Our task is to listen for Him and follow His directions. Continued guidance, a satisfied soul, His strength—what wonderful promises for life!

The LORD will guide you continually,
And satisfy your soul in drought,
And strengthen your bones;
You shall be like a watered garden,
And like a spring of water, whose waters do not fail.

Isaiah 58:11

I will instruct you and teach you in
the way you should go;
I will guide you with My eye.

Psalm 32:8

"When He, the Spirit of truth, has come,
He will guide you into all truth; for He
will not speak on His own authority,
but whatever He hears He will speak;
and He will tell you things to
come."

John 16:13

Stand Firm

I gave My back to those who struck Me,
And My cheeks to those who plucked out the beard;
I did not hide My face from shame and spitting.

Isaiah 50:6

*C*hristmas can bring out the best in people. We see the so-called Christmas spirit evident in people's thoughtfulness, courtesy, and graciousness to one another. We witness acts of sacrificial generosity and Christlike kindness.

Sadly, however, Christmas can also bring out the worst in people. As we go about our days, we see people being rude, fighting over limited stock in stores, or blatantly disrespecting others.

In Isaiah's day, disrespect was a serious offense. Pulling someone's beard, for instance, was not only a sign of contempt but also the highest insult. As Isaiah prophesied, the Messiah—God's Chosen One— would be treated with utter disrespect, yet Jesus would not hide His face or turn from the humiliation and shame. What a strong and humble Savior.

Not in Vain

—— ✳ ——

Then [the members of the Sanhedrin] spat in [Jesus'] face and beat Him; and others struck Him with the palms of their hands, saying, "Prophesy to us, Christ! Who is the one who struck You?"

Matthew 26:67–68

*H*ave you noticed the common story line for most superheroes? They come from humble beginnings, they are humiliated or made fun of by their peers, but they use their strength to overcome circumstances and help others.

Now consider the life of Jesus. Beginnings don't come much humbler than being laid in a feeding trough as a baby. Humiliation can't get much worse than dying a totally undeserved death on a cross. Jesus could have overcome the Roman soldiers at any point, but He didn't. Why? Because He chose to use His strength not to resist His tormentors but instead to fulfill God's plan, prophesied centuries before, to bring us salvation. Jesus overcame not His oppressors, but rather sin and death—*our oppressors.* And Jesus overcame not to free Himself, but to free us to share eternity with Him.

His Strength

~~ ✻ ~~

*G*od promises His people strength—the kind of strength Jesus showed as He let Himself be nailed to the cross in submission to God's plan. Even though we know God's immeasurable strength is available to us, our fear—of Satan, of spiritual warfare, or simply of the unknown—may still be very real.

Consider these truths with which you can counter those fears: God is all-powerful. His strength is available 24/7. Whatever our situation, God goes before us, and He is always with us. Nothing is impossible for God. We can accomplish all He asks of us as long as we rely on His strength instead of our own. Even though circumstances of life might appear overwhelming, they are no match for our Savior.

The apparently helpless Babe born in Bethlehem was actually our omnipotent, almighty God in human flesh. In a Christmas card, point someone who needs hope and strength to Him, to the Shield and Refuge, to the Savior.

The Lord is my strength and my shield;
My heart trusted in Him, and I am helped;
Therefore my heart greatly rejoices,
And with my song I will praise Him.
The Lord is their strength,
And He is the saving refuge of His anointed.
Save Your people,
And bless Your inheritance;
Shepherd them also,
And bear them up forever.

Psalm 28:7–9

I can do all things through Christ who
strengthens me.

Philippians 4:13

The Lord is my light and my salvation;
Whom shall I fear?
The Lord is the strength of my life;
Of whom shall I be afraid?

Psalm 27:1

Paid in Full

—✳—

*He shall see the labor of His soul, and be
    satisfied.
By His knowledge My righteous Servant shall
    justify many,
For He shall bear their iniquities.
Therefore I will divide Him a portion with the
    great,
And He shall divide the spoil with the strong,
Because He poured out His soul unto death,
And He was numbered with the transgressors,
And He bore the sin of many,
And made intercession for the transgressors.*

Isaiah 53:11–12

*I*saiah 53 is the prophet's "Servant Song," and in it Isaiah offers a description of the promised Messiah.

- This coming Messiah will deliver Israel and establish justice for all.
- The Messiah will be wise.
- The Messiah will suffer and die.

Isaiah prophesied that Jesus would be "numbered with the transgressors": the sinless Christ would be treated as a sinner. He would die, however, on behalf of our sins, not His. And with His death, the prophet proclaimed, Jesus would pay the debt of sin for all of humanity.

Among Thieves

~ ✳ ~

With [Jesus] they also crucified two robbers, one on His right and the other on His left. So the Scripture was fulfilled which says, "And He was numbered with the transgressors."

Mark 15:27–28

Then one of the criminals who were hanged blasphemed Him, saying, "If You are the Christ, save Yourself and us."

But the other [thief], answering, rebuked him, saying, "Do you not even fear God, seeing you are under the same condemnation? And we indeed justly, for we receive the due reward of our deeds; but this Man has done nothing wrong." Then he said to Jesus, "Lord, remember me when You come into Your kingdom."

And Jesus said to him, "Assuredly, I say to you, today you will be with Me in Paradise."

Luke 23:39–43

*C*ommunication is complicated for many reasons. Have you noticed, for instance, that two people can hear the same message yet come away with different interpretations?

On Golgotha stood three crosses, and Jesus hung on the one in the center, between two thieves. Both thieves heard the jeering of the crowd, and both read the sign intended to mock Jesus: "THIS IS THE KING OF THE JEWS" (Luke 23:38). One thief added his insults to the crowd's; the other, however, came to Jesus' defense. Why? Because the second thief realized what every follower of Christ needs to acknowledge.

- First, I am guilty of sin; Jesus is innocent.
- Second, Jesus is not on the cross for His sins; He is there for mine.

Jesus was "numbered among transgressors"! Isaiah's prophecy was fulfilled for our benefit. What an extravagant gift!

His Compassion

～ ✳ ～

*M*ortgages, car loans, credit cards—we may feel as though we can never cover all our debts! One of our debts, however, has been paid in full by One who was not in debt at all. When He hung on the cross, was buried, and rose victorious three days later, the sinless Jesus fully paid the sin debt of every human being. Something we could never repay on our own merit, Jesus repaid *completely*. What an act of infinite compassion and incomparable love! Throughout the Gospels, Jesus demonstrated through miracles and taught in parables God's divine compassion and love. What will you do this Christmas season to show someone God's compassion and love and thereby the hope of Christmas?

Who is a God like You,
Pardoning iniquity
And passing over the transgression of the remnant of
His heritage?

He does not retain His anger forever,
Because He delights in mercy.
He will again have compassion on us,
And will subdue our iniquities.

You will cast all our sins
Into the depths of the sea.

Micah 7:18–19

When [Jesus] saw the multitudes, He was
moved with compassion for them, because
they were weary and scattered, like sheep
having no shepherd.

Matthew 9:36

When Jesus went out He saw a great
multitude; and He was moved with
compassion for them, and healed
their sick.

Matthew 14:14

They Cast Lots

~~~ ✳ ~~~

I can count all My bones.
They look and stare at Me.
They divide My garments among them,
And for My clothing they cast lots.

Psalm 22:17–18

*Q*uick! Say the first thing that comes to mind. A classic Christmas story? Dickens's *A Christmas Carol.* A favorite Christmas movie? *It's a Wonderful Life.* A favorite Old Testament hero? David—shepherd, king, songwriter. In fact, David wrote many psalms. In some, he praised God for His love, guidance, and care. In others, as in Psalm 22, David cried out to God in distress. Despairing and in danger, he believed that if God didn't act, he would die. David wasn't intentionally being prophetic, but interestingly, all four gospel writers quoted verse 18 when they described Jesus' crucifixion. Clearly, they felt that David's words aptly represented our Savior's pain on His final day on earth. Similarly, the angels' song from Jesus' first day on this planet may put words to your Christmas joy: "Glory to God in the highest!"

Sticks and Stones

Jesus said, "Father, forgive them, for they do not know what they do."

And they divided His garments and cast lots. . . . But even the rulers with them sneered, saying, "He saved others; let Him save Himself if He is the Christ, the chosen of God."

Luke 23:34–35

Sticks and stones may break my bones . . ." True. "But words will never hurt me." Far from true! Hurtful words cut to the heart, and there, at the site of Jesus' crucifixion, came bitter, sarcastic words. Hadn't Jesus suffered enough?

As David's psalm had foreshadowed, the Roman guards cast lots for Jesus' clothing. Stripped of His robe, His dignity, and soon His life, Jesus nevertheless asked His Father to forgive the very men who were spewing hurtful remarks and gambling for His clothes.

Yet Jesus offered undeserved forgiveness, and He offers the same to you and me.

His Forgiveness

~~ ❋ ~~

*P*aul was a man transformed by God's for-giveness. This good Jew spent the first part of his life persecuting fellow Jews who believed in Jesus—but that was before the risen Lord met him and changed him on the Damascus Road. That began his tutorial in how to live for God.

As Paul later taught, God wants every part of us—body, soul, and spirit—to enter into relationship with Him and to focus on growing close to Him. And because God wants no barriers between us, He will forgive all our sins, and He promises to remember them no more. The forgiveness God has promised to us is irrevocable; when we are genuinely repentant, we receive it.

One more thing: you just may need to seek forgive-ness from someone in your circle of family, friends, neighbors, and acquaintances. Remember, it will be a Christmas gift to both of you.

Lord, hear my voice!
Let Your ears be attentive
To the voice of my supplications.

If You, LORD, should mark iniquities,
O Lord, who could stand?
But there is forgiveness with You,
That You may be feared.

I wait for the LORD, my soul waits,
And in His word I do hope.

Psalm 130:2–5

You, being dead in your trespasses and the
uncircumcision of your flesh, [Jesus] has
made alive together with Him, having
forgiven you all trespasses, having wiped
out the handwriting of requirements that
was against us, which was contrary
to us. And He has taken it out of the
way, having nailed it to the cross.

Colossians 2:13–14

God Delivers the Righteous

~~✳~~

The eyes of the LORD are on the righteous,
And His ears are open to their cry.
The face of the LORD is against those who do evil,
To cut off the remembrance of them from the
     earth.
The righteous cry out, and the LORD hears,
And delivers them out of all their troubles.
The LORD is near to those who have a broken
     heart,
And saves such as have a contrite spirit.

Many are the afflictions of the righteous,
But the LORD delivers him out of them all.
He guards all his bones;
Not one of them is broken.

Psalm 34:15–20

*H*ave you ever purchased a Christmas gift from the electronics department and been asked, "Do you want the protection plan that goes with it?" God is our very own protection plan. No matter what circumstances we find ourselves in, God is willing—and eager—to guide our steps, protect us, and deliver us. If we are faithful to Him and are doing our best to follow His plan for our lives, He promises to deliver us.

"But the cross?" you ask.

God let Christ die. Did the Lord—as this psalm proclaims—hear Jesus' cry? Did He hear our righteous Savior's cry? Did He deliver Jesus out of all His troubles and afflictions? Did He guard Jesus' bones so that not one of them was broken? Which parts of these verses are prophetic?

No Bones Broken

~~~ ❋ ~~~

Because it was the Preparation Day, that the bodies should not remain on the cross on the Sabbath (for that Sabbath was a high day), the Jews asked Pilate that their legs might be broken, and that they might be taken away. Then the soldiers came and broke the legs of the first and of the other who was crucified with Him. But when they came to Jesus and saw that He was already dead, they did not break His legs. . . . For these things were done that the Scripture should be fulfilled, "Not one of His bones shall be broken."

John 19:31–33, 36

Fulfillment

*I*t was Friday of Passover week, the day before the Sabbath, and celebrations and festivities were going on throughout Jerusalem. Yet just a short distance away, three men had been executed. According to Jewish ceremonial law, bodies of executed criminals had to be removed before sunset (Deuteronomy 21:23). So the Jews went to Pilate and requested that the deaths of the three men be hastened by breaking their legs. Pilate granted their request. But when the soldiers got to Jesus, He was already dead. His legs didn't need to be broken. Prophecy fulfilled: God had not allowed His Son's bones to be broken.

His Mercy

~※~

For every action there is an equal but opposite reaction. This is Sir Isaac Newton's Third Law of Motion and a basic principle of physics. Does it apply in the spiritual realm?

God freely gives us His mercy: an *action*. And what is our *reaction* to His action? Praise—and may it be equal to the weight of His mercy in our lives!

It is God's very nature to give His children mercy and grace—but not because we deserve it. "His mercy endures forever"—and forever is a long time. There is no expiration date. Why does God do this for us? Simply because He loves us.

God sends a sunrise every morning, He listens when we talk, and He gave us His only Son at Christmas. How can we react to God's infinitely gracious actions? With our praises. By worshiping Him with all our heart, soul, mind, and strength. No, that reaction can never equal God's generosity; thankfully, He is more concerned about our hearts than about the laws of physics.

Oh, give thanks to the Lord, *for He is good!*
For His mercy endures forever.
Let the redeemed of the Lord *say so,*
Whom He has redeemed from the hand of the enemy,
And gathered out of the lands,
From the east and from the west,
From the north and from the south.

Psalm 107:1–3

Praise the Lord!

Oh, give thanks to the Lord, *for He is*
good!
For His mercy endures forever.

Who can utter the mighty acts of the
Lord?
Who can declare all His praise?
Blessed are those who keep justice,
And he who does righteousness at
all times!

Psalm 106:1–3

Buried with the Rich

$\sim$ ✳ $\sim$

They made His grave with the wicked—
But with the rich at His death,
Because He had done no violence,
Nor was any deceit in His mouth.

Isaiah 53:9

*I*saiah's prophecy offers insight into how the coming Messiah would be treated, and the truth was jarring. The long-awaited Messiah would receive no respect. His burial would be common; His grave would be with the wicked. Yet Isaiah closed the passage with a glimmer of hope: Jesus would be "with the rich at His death." The remainder of verse 9 explains why: Christ's death was undeserved. An utterly innocent Man died for your sins and mine.

Treated with Respect

*When evening had come, there came a rich man
from Arimathea, named Joseph, who himself had
also become a disciple of Jesus. This man went to
Pilate and asked for the body of Jesus. Then Pilate
commanded the body to be given to him. When Joseph
had taken the body, he wrapped it in a clean linen
cloth, and laid it in his new tomb ... and he rolled a
large stone against the door of the tomb, and departed.*

Matthew 27:57–60

A secret follower of Christ, Joseph of Arimathea boldly stepped forward at his Lord's death and asked to bury the body. Courage replaced fear; Joseph's faith was no longer a secret. After receiving permission from Pilate, Jesus' body was wrapped in clean linen and spices. Joseph had decided to give his own tomb to Jesus, a small but compassionate act of love. And with this gesture, Joseph fulfilled Isaiah's prophecy that the Messiah would be buried with the rich. A Roman guard stood at the entrance. For three days, no one went near the grave.

Abundance from Above

*O*pportunities to give are all around us, more at this time of the year than at any other. Do you feel a pang of guilt that you can't do more? Or, on a smaller scale, if you receive a gift and don't have one to give in return? We selfish, self-centered human beings expect our giving to be reciprocated. Why give if we have nothing to gain?

God, however, has a very different take on giving, because divine love is different. Christlike love gives unselfishly and expects nothing in return. Yet because we love God, we want to respond to His gifts. Oh, there is no way we could ever repay all He has given to us, but we can give to others our talents, energy, time, and money to demonstrate God's love in our lives—and pay it forward. To whom—and how—will you pay forward God's unselfish love this season?

Promise

Let each one give as he purposes in his heart, not grudgingly or of necessity; for God loves a cheerful giver. And God is able to make all grace abound toward you, that you, always having all sufficiency in all things, may have an abundance for every good work.

2 Corinthians 9:7–8

For you know the grace of our Lord Jesus Christ, that though He was rich, yet for your sakes He became poor, that you through His poverty might become rich.

2 Corinthians 8:9

Delivered from Death

———❋———

You will show me the path of life;
In Your presence is fullness of joy;
At Your right hand are pleasures forevermore. . . .
But God will redeem my soul from the power of
     the grave,
For He shall receive me.

Psalm 16:11; 49:15

Ebenezer Scrooge is a greedy man who despises Christmas. As his redemption story unfolds in *A Christmas Carol*, Scrooge is visited by three ghosts. He listens to what each has to say, and the fear of his own death and his concern about the legacy and reputation he will leave seem to spark him to change his ways. A glimpse of eternity makes a difference.

The psalmist also gives us a glimpse of eternity, prophesying that God "will redeem my soul from the power of the grave." In what ways and for whom will that prophecy prove true? The answer may prompt this glimpse of eternity to make a difference in your life and mine.

"He Is Not Here"

Entering the tomb, [the women] saw a young man clothed in a long white robe sitting on the right side . . .

But he said to them, "Do not be alarmed. You seek Jesus of Nazareth, who was crucified. He is risen! He is not here. See the place where they laid Him. But go, tell His disciples—and Peter—that He is going before you into Galilee; there you will see Him, as He said to you."

Mark 16:5–7

The past few days had been emotionally draining: Jesus, their Lord, had died. Mary Magdalene had watched to see where His body would be taken. After another sleepless night, Mary rose before the sun and met the others. As they made their way to where Jesus lay, they wondered how they would move the heavy stone blocking the entrance to the tomb. Yet when they rounded the last corner, the stone had already been rolled away!

Fearfully, they entered the tomb, but instead of Jesus' body, they saw an angel who said, "He is risen!" God had—as Isaiah prophesied—redeemed Jesus from the power of the grave. And that truth gives us hope, for Christmas and for eternity.

Fulfillment

Eternal Life

———— ✳ ————

*E*arly-bird specials. Door-busters. Lowest-price-of-the-season sales. The ads are everywhere—but what if you came across one that said, "Free Ticket to Heaven"? You check the fine print: "Limited time offer. Must redeem before you die. Sinners only."

Of course, you don't need a ticket to enter heaven, but Jesus, by His sacrificial death on the cross for our sins, does offer the gift of eternal life to all of us sinners, and we do need to receive it before we die. Now, eternal life doesn't mean we simply go to heaven and live forever, although that alone would be spectacular. It means we enjoy an eternal friendship with Jesus—starting the very moment we accept Him as Savior! We will continue in heaven the relationship with Jesus that we begin here.

Sharing your excitement about your friendship with the Savior will lead others to wonder what is different about your life and to want it for themselves. They will find in Jesus the gift of eternal life (it begins now) and the hope of Christmas (it lasts forever).

Having been set free from sin, and having become slaves of God, you have your fruit to holiness, and the end, everlasting life. For the wages of sin is death, but the gift of God is eternal life in Christ Jesus our Lord.

Romans 6:22–23

Let that abide in you which you heard from the beginning. If what you heard from the beginning abides in you, you also will abide in the Son and in the Father. And this is the promise that He has promised us— eternal life. . . . And this is the testimony: that God has given us eternal life, and this life is in His Son. He who has the Son has life; he who does not have the Son of God does not have life.

1 John 2:24–25; 5:11–12

CHRIST THE LORD *Is* RISEN TODAY

CHARLES WESLEY

Christ the Lord is risen today, Alleluia!
Sons of men and angels say, Alleluia!
Raise your joys and triumphs high, Alleluia!
Sing, ye heavens, and earth, reply, Alleluia!

Lives again our glorious King, Alleluia!
Where, O death, is now thy sting? Alleluia!
Once He died our souls to save, Alleluia!
Where thy victory, O grave? Alleluia!

Love's redeeming work is done, Alleluia!
Fought the fight, the battle won, Alleluia!
Death in vain forbids Him rise, Alleluia!
Christ has opened paradise, Alleluia!

Soar we now where Christ has led, Alleluia!
Following our exalted Head, Alleluia!
Made like Him, like Him we rise, Alleluia!
Ours the cross, the grave, the skies, Alleluia!

Right Hand of God

———※———

The LORD said to my Lord,
"Sit at My right hand,
Till I make Your enemies Your footstool."

Psalm 110:1

he seat at someone's right hand was a place of great honor. But who is extending to whom the honor mentioned in the prophetic Psalm 110:1?

David's first use of the word *LORD* clearly refers to God. The second use—*my Lord*—is David's respectful reference to someone higher ranking than he was. The backstory of this verse is the prophecy that God will send One who would first be victorious over sin and then sit next to Him in heaven. And what does the prophecy say will result? Fellowship between God and His people.

Received into Heaven

After the Lord had spoken to [the eleven remaining disciples], He was received up into heaven, and sat down at the right hand of God. And they went out and preached everywhere.

Mark 16:19–20

*T*he promised Holy Spirit had not yet come, and the eleven disciples did not yet fully grasp the nature and scope of Jesus' mission. They wanted to know when Christ would restore the kingdom of Israel as prophesied. But Jesus told them that the Father alone knows the time. Then, after commanding His followers to go into all the world as His witnesses, Jesus was taken up into heaven in a cloud, where He is, as David also said, at God's right hand.

Jesus still sits at the right hand of the Father to make intercession for each of us. Although Jesus' work on earth is done, His ministry continues through us. You and I are to continue sharing His message of Christmas hope with the hopeless world.

The Holy Spirit

With a sound like a violent wind and amid flames of fire, the long-promised Holy Spirit arrived on the day of Pentecost. The disciples and other Christ-followers witnessed His undeniable presence and continue to do so even today as He gives comfort, wisdom, and power to those who name Jesus as their Lord and Savior.

Once we name Jesus as Lord and receive His Spirit, we then choose daily—if not moment by moment—whether to live in the Spirit, whether to depend on His power, follow His direction, and rely on Him to help us die to self. When we make that choice to walk with the Spirit—when we choose to let Him guide us along the narrow path of loving, joyful, and free-ing friendship with Christ—others will glimpse in us what God is like. And by the Spirit's power, we can resist the temptations of the world, stand strong in God's truth, keep our eyes on the Lord Jesus, and know in our heart of hearts *the hope of Christmas*.

"The Helper, the Holy Spirit, whom the Father will send in My name, He will teach you all things, and bring to your remembrance all things that I said to you."

John 14:26

"You shall receive power when the Holy Spirit has come upon you; and you shall be witnesses to Me in Jerusalem, and in all Judea and Samaria, and to the end of the earth." . . . And when they had prayed, the place where they were assembled together was shaken; and they were all filled with the Holy Spirit, and they spoke the word of God with boldness.

Acts 1:8; 4:31

JOY
to the
WORLD

ISAAC WATTS

Joy to the world, the Lord is come! Let earth
*   receive her King.*
Let every heart prepare Him room,
And heaven and nature sing, and heaven and
*   nature sing,*
And heaven, and heaven and nature sing.

Joy to the earth, the Savior reigns! Let men
*   their songs employ,*
While fields and floods, rocks, hills and plains
Repeat the sounding joy, repeat the sounding
*   joy,*
Repeat, repeat the sounding joy.

No more let sin and sorrow grow, nor thorns
*   infest the ground.*
He comes to make His blessings flow
Far as the curse is found, far as the curse is
*   found,*
Far as, far as the curse is found.

He rules the world with truth and grace and
*   makes the nations prove*
The glories of His righteousness
And wonders of His love, and wonders of His
*   love,*
And wonders, and wonders of His love.

The Gift of Prayer

❧✳❧

*T*hroughout the Bible, God promises to speak to His children, but we must listen for His voice. Key to such active listening is going before the Lord expectantly. Eagerly anticipating His words to us will prime our hearts and minds to hear Him. And this kind of prayer dialogue is essential to our relationship with God—the Almighty One who knows our names and numbers the hairs on our heads. All-loving and utterly compassionate, He desires to have us share with Him our innermost thoughts and feelings, our dreams and fears, our regrets and hopes. Our Creator God—our heavenly Father—wants to hear from us when the road is rough as well as when it is smooth. Sweet times of prayer happen when we go before Him with praise, worshiping and giving thanks for what He has done. Prayer is the breath of our spiritual life. We can go to God as often as we like each day, and we will be blessed.

"Call to Me, and I will answer you, and show you great and mighty things, which you do not know."

Jeremiah 33:3

Be anxious for nothing, but in everything by prayer and supplication, with thanksgiving, let your requests be made known to God; and the peace of God, which surpasses all understanding, will guard your hearts and minds through Christ Jesus.

Philippians 4:6–7

Now may the Lord of peace Himself give you peace always in every way. The Lord be with you all. . . .
The grace of our Lord Jesus Christ be with you all. Amen.

2 Thessalonians 3:16, 18

Confess your trespasses to one another, and pray for one another, that you may be healed. The effective, fervent prayer of a righteous man avails much.

James 5:16